SILENT SIGNALS
UNLOCKING COMMUNICATION WITH
ECHONOSE

by
Benjami
David

Copyright © 2024
by **Benjamin David**
All rights reserved. No part of this book may be reproduced in any manner whatsoever without written permission except in the case of brief quotations embodied in critical articles and reviews.
First Printing, 2024

ABSTRACT

EchoNose is a minimally-invasive wearable device capable of detecting silent speech words and articulators (such as tongue movement) using active acoustic sensing through the nasal cavity. This effect is possible due to the interconnectivity of the upper respiratory tract cavities. We explore the feasibility of EchoNose by (1) continuously tracking speech articulators using an electromagnetic articulograph (EMA) for ground truth, and (2) conducting a silent speech user study with 6 participants comparing EchoNose against CV performance on a list of 21 common words and 10 "tongue-specific" words.

Contents

SECTION 1 : INTRODUCTION 1
Section 2 : Related Works 3
SECTION 3 : Stationary SSR Systems 5
SECTION 4 : CV Approach 5
SECTION 5 : Wearable SSR Systems 7
SECTION 6 : *Theory of Operation* 12
SECTION 7 : Upper Respiratory Tract Anatomy 14
SECTION 8 : Implementation 20
Preliminary Experiments 26
SECTION 8 : EMA Experiment - Continuously Tracking Speech Articulators 33
Session 9 - Wordlist Axes Extraction 44
Session 10 - Tongue Movement Axes Extraction 45
Session 11 - Wordlist Articulator Predictions 47
SECTION 12 : Tongue Tip 48
SECTION 13 : Silent Speech User Study 55
Low performance in the early sessions - we doubled the length of the practice session to allow users to gain more familiarity with the data collection process before beginning the first session 61
the following section - "User Study Design") 61
labials - 64
rounded lip sounds 64
voiced consonant counterparts - 65
open vowels. 65

SECTION 1 : INTRODUCTION

Silent speech recognition (SSR) is a useful tool for two primary purposes. Firstly, SSR systems have the ability to assist users who suffer from speech disorders such as vocal fold paralysis or speech impediment issues. Secondly, SSR interfaces have the potential to offer novel human-computer input options to users in the future. Wearable devices aimed at both applications have penetrated the SSR space, offering additional convenience and portability to users. However, this often comes at the cost of lower performance when compared to stationary systems (such as MRI, EMG, EMA, ultrasound, or frontal camera CV approaches). The vast majority of wearable devices in the SSR space evaluate their system by performing discrete classification on a list of application-specific words. Wearables with the ability to detect more fine-grained speech activities such as phonemes or speech articulator positions (e.g. tongue tracking) either require inside-the-mouth sensors or heavy instrumentation. There is therefore a need for a minimally-intrusive, higher performing wearable device capable of not only classifying discrete words, but also recognizing more fine grained speech activities such as tongue movement. EchoNose aims to fill this gap by introducing a novel SSR approach that leverages the interconnectivity of the upper respiratory tract cavities to recognize SSR activities through the nose using active acoustic sensing. First, we explore the feasibility of EchoNose to continuously track speech articulators using an electromagnetic articulograph (EMA) machine as ground truth. Secondly, we test EchoNose's ability to classify 21 function words and 10 linguistically similar words in a user study consisting of 6 participants, and compare the results against CV performance. Finally, we lead a discussion on the feasibility of using EchoNose for various applications in the future and the challenges and limitations thereof.

Section 2 :Related Works

Many researchers have successfully built silent speech recognition (SSR) systems capable of recognizing silent speech words and articulators (such as the tongue). Silent speech recognition systems can be divided into two main groups: (1) stationary systems, and (2) wearable systems. Stationary systems tend to offer higher performance, while wearable devices offer more convenience and portability to users. Wearable systems can be divided into two subgroups as well: (1) in-mouth sensing wearables, and (2) external sensing wearables. In-mouth sensing wearables are able to track more fine-grained speech activities such as tongue movement, but are naturally more invasive. External sensing wearables require no such instrumentation, and are therefore less invasive. However, these systems are typically unable to track more fine-grained speech activities such as tongue movement. There is therefore a need for an outside-the-mouth wearable device, capable of tracking inside-the-mouth speech activities such as tongue movement. EchoNose leverages the interconnectivity of the nasal cavity and the oral cavity to detect such activities by passing active acoustic signals through the nose.

Section 3 : Stationary SSR Systems

Some researchers have explored using highly invasive stationary sensing methods such as MRI or ultrasound machines to recognize silent speech. Stationary (or non-wearable) SSR systems have access to high resolution data of the oral tract, and are therefore able to achieve more impressive results - at the expense of portability and convenience. In 2021, Pandey and Sabbir created a speech to text interface using real time MRI image frames. Other projects such as Kimura, Kono, and Rekimoto's in 2019 built similar systems using ultrasound imaging instead. The models proposed in these projects demonstrate that given a rich enough dataset, silent
speech to text interfaces are feasible. However, the instruments necessary to acquire such a dataset are large, expensive and impractical.

Section 4 : CV Approach

The frontal camera (CV) approach to SSR aims to

strike a balance between performance and practicality. Due to the large number of video recordings available of people speaking, coupled with advancements in computer vision, the CV ("lip reading") approach is one of the most extensively explored methods in the SSR space. Some examples of CV systems include LipNet (Assael, Shillingford, Whiteson and Nando de Freitasin, 2016), Improved Speech Reconstruction from Silent Video (Ephrat, Halperin, Peleg, 2017), the work on long short-term memory of Wand in 2016, and Updating the Silent Speech Challenge benchmark with deep learning (Ji, Yana, and Liu, 2018). CV models are able to achieve impressive accuracies classifying silent speech words. However, they struggle to distinguish between certain groups of similar phonemes, called visemes (e.g. [/t/, /n/, /l/] or [/w/, /r/]). Visemes are sets of sounds that visually appear the same from outside the mouth. Frontal camera CV systems rely heavily on lip movement and jaw movement to detect speech words, since tongue movement is relatively hidden from view. The tongue, however, is arguably the most important speech articulator. It can move across many degrees of freedom and is involved in the production of nearly all speech sounds. For this reason, tongue-blind SSR systems, no matter how optimized, will always be limited in their ability to recognize silent speech. Additionally, frontal cameras are impractical in free living environments when hands are occupied or mobility is a priority.

SECTION 5 : Wearable SSR Systems

Wearable SSR Systems aim to offer increased portability to users, so that silent speech commands can be recognized in mobile settings. However, this added convenience of portability often comes at the expense of performance. Some wearable devices are more invasive, requiring inside-the-mouth sensors or heavy instrumentation of the head. These devices are typically capable of more fine-grained speech recognition such as tongue tracking. Other wearables prioritize convenience and require less invasive instrumentation measures. We have thus divided SSR wearables into two groups: (1) wearables that require sensors inside the mouth, and (2) wearables that do not require sensors inside the mouth (the former being generally more invasive than the latter).

Wearables using In-Mouth Sensors

Many wearable systems rely on sensors inside the mouth to track speech articulators (namely the tongue). Fagan in 2008 developed an SSR wearable device capable of recognizing 9 silent words and 13 silent phonemes using magnetic sensing. The mask frame form factor housed 6 magnetometers which tracked 7 permanent magnets attached to the tongue and lips. In 2014, Sahni built a device based on Tongue Drive which combines a "Tongue Magnet Interface" (using just one magnet) with an ear interface to classify one of 11 phrases. In order for these interfaces to work, permanent magnets must first be pierced or glued to the tongue, which is an invasive process. Other researchers[1] have explored using a retainer form factor instead. In 2019, the work of Li, Wu and Starner in Tongueboard presented a retainer device capable of recognizing 21 words with an average accuracy of 91% for native speakers and 78% for non-native speakers.

The retainer was capable of recognizing four tongue swiping gestures as well. Like Tongueboard,

[1] Such as Saponas, Kelly, Parviz, and Tan in 2009, Hashimoto in 2018 or Li, Wu and Starner in 2019.

EchoNose also aims to recognize silent speech commands with a secondary focus on tongue movement. Therefore, due to the hybrid nature of both projects, we chose to adopt Tongueboard's wordlist (21 words) verbatim into our own user study as a baseline dataset.

Wearables using External Sensors

Many previous wearables have successfully recognized silent speech without the need for in-mouth instrumentation. For instance, Schultz in 2010, Toth in 2009 and Kapur in 2008 explored using electromyography (EMG) to convert silent speech utterances into voice. These systems are often able to achieve higher performances than other external sensing methods, but are highly invasive, requiring that multiple surface electrodes be stuck to the face and neck. Due to the laborious nature of remounting (taking off and putting back on) EMG electrodes, session dependency is a severe limitation. Other projects such as SottoVoce (Kimura, Kono and Rekimoto in 2019) and DNN (Csapo, Gabor, Grosz, Gosztolya, Toth and Marko in 2017) used ultrasonic sensing to detect silent speech activity. However, like EMG, this method also involves heavy instrumentation, requiring users to wear an obtrusive helmet or be accompanied by large machinery. C-Face (T. Chen, 2020) and Speechin (R. Zhang, 2021) propose a less invasive external sensing approach for silent speech recognition. Their approach uses small cameras embedded in a wearable device to detect subtle skin deformations of the cheeks or chin to classify silent speech words. They are both minimally invasive and session independent. However, they are limited in their ability to detect tongue movement. EchoNose seeks to fill this void by presenting a minimally invasive, session independent wearable device focused on detecting inside-the-mouth speech activities such as tongue movement.

SECTION 6 : *Theory of Operation*

The EchoNose theory of operation involves an intersection of four key concepts: (1) active acoustic sensing, (2) upper respiratory tract anatomy, (3) source filter theory, and (4) silent speech recognition. The following section introduces each concept and explains how they converge to form the theory of operation behind EchoNose.

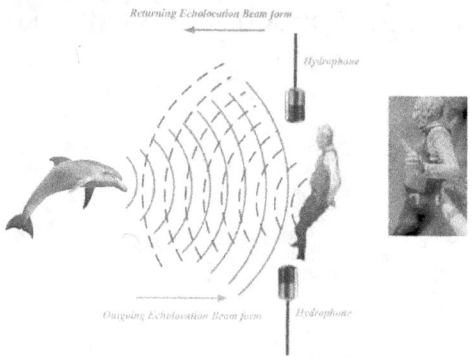

Active Acoustic Sensing

Active acoustic sensing is a mode of detecting the environment by which sound is generated from a speaker and reflected signals are then captured with a microphone. Based on the shape and distance of objects in the environment, the signals propagate in unique patterns. Machine learning models can then recognize these patterns and map them to events taking place in the environment. Dolphins use a similar method called echolocation to "see" underwater (see figure 1).

Figure 1: A dolphin echolocation algorithm [2]

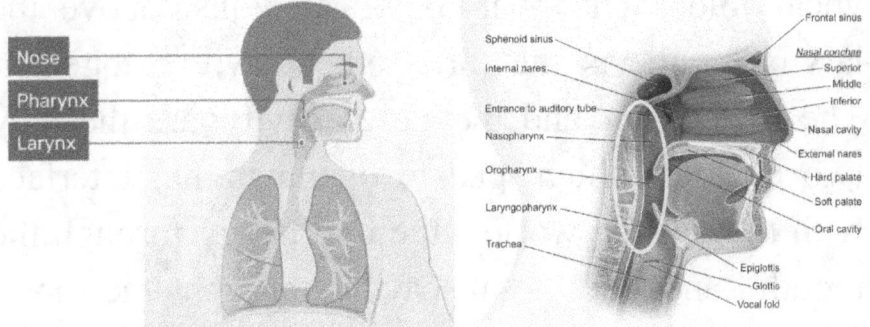

Section 7: Upper Respiratory Tract Anatomy

The upper respiratory tract is composed of four interconnected cavities: the nasal cavity, the oral cavity, the pharynx and the larynx (see figure 2). The larynx is the bottommost cavity and houses the vocal folds. The pharynx, located just above the larynx, connects the three other cavities together. The oral cavity and the nasal cavity are the only two cavities which lead to openings that interface with the outside world - the oral cavity through the mouth, and the nasal cavity through the nose. Although most speech sounds travel out the mouth, a subset of speech sounds called nasals (such as /m/, /n/, or /ng/) propagate out the nose instead.

Figure 2: left image: the fully respiratory system, right image: the pharynx (circled in blue) connects the nasal cavity to the oral cavity [3, 4]

Source Filter Theory

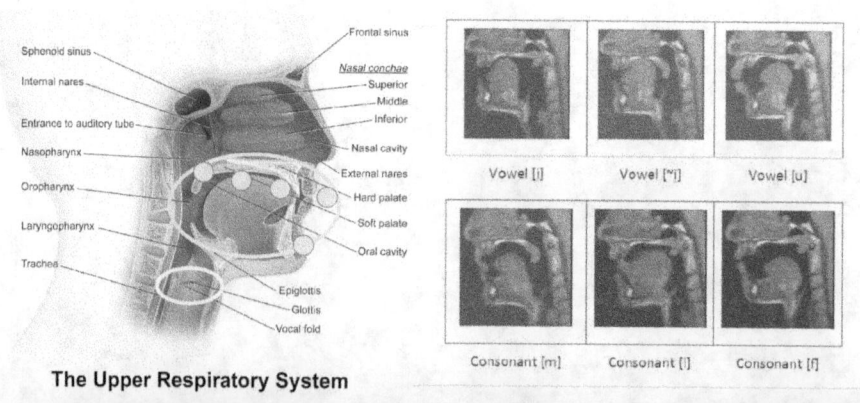

"Source Filter Theory" is a simplified model in phonetics of the relation between speech acoustics and articulation, which separates speech production into two parts: the source and the filter. The source of speech production is the vocal folds. The human vocal folds typically vibrate
in the 100-200 Hz range, depending on a number of factors such as age and sex. Vocal folds send acoustic signals up the pharynx, into the oral cavity and out the mouth (or nose for nasals). The filter of speech production is the oral cavity. As the oral cavity changes shape, acoustic signals from the vocal folds attenuate in different patterns, hence the "filtering" effect. Speech articulators are the parts of the mouth that move to change the shape of the oral cavity (the filter). The primary speech articulators include the lips, jaw, tongue tip, tongue body, velum and glottis.

Figure 3: Left image: The Upper Respiratory system showing the vocal folds (source) circled in yellow and the oral tract (filter) circled in green. Green dots represent speech articulators. Right image: the filter changes shape in the production of various speech sounds. [5, 6]

A "Second Source" for Silent Speech

The challenge that silent speech recognition (SSR) systems face is how to recognize what the filter (oral tract) is doing, without any help from the source (vocal folds). It's important to note at this time that there are also other sources in phonetics, such as fricative sounds or plosives but those sources are typically not addressed in silent speech projects. In vocalized speech, acoustic signals reach the oral tract through the lower pharynx. The nasal cavity is connected to the oral cavity through the upper pharynx. This raises the question, if a second artificial source were introduced passing sound through the nose, could the reflected signals capture information about the filter? This approach is similar to how regular speech works, except that instead of the vocal folds sending low frequency acoustic signals through the lower pharynx and into the oral cavity, the ultrasonic speaker would instead access the oral cavity through the nasal cavity at a much higher frequency of 19-23 kHz (see figure 4).

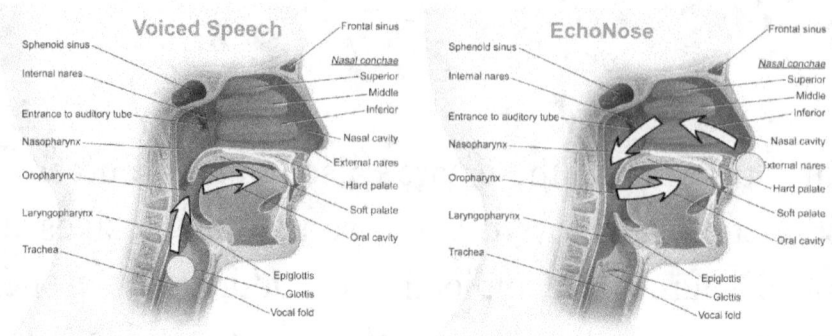

Figure 4: The light blue circle represents the vocal folds on the left, and the EchoNose speaker on the right [7]

With a microphone and speaker positioned under each nostril, as the shape of the oral cavity (or filter) changes during speech, one could expect reflected acoustic signals from the speaker to change as well. These attenuations could then be picked up by the microphone, and machine learning could be used to detect patterns in the signals and recognize silent speech. The question is whether or not high-frequency active acoustic signals propagated through the nose contain enough information to detect tongue position or other oral articulators. To answer this question we created a wearable device and conducted several preliminary experiments.

Section 8: Implementation

In this section we describe how we implemented EchoNose in three parts: (1) form factor design,

(2) hardware, and (3) signal processing. In short, we built a mask form factor, which positioned a single microphone and speaker below each nostril, and used a frequency modulated continuous wave (FMCW) for signal processing.

Form Factor Design

The goal of the form factor was to create a minimally intrusive design, capable of adapting to different face shapes and sizes. The EchoNose form factor underwent three phases of evolution (see Figure 5). The first was a small 3D printed nose "cap" which was secured to the user's nose using two elastic bands borrowed from an n95 mask. The second was a more complex, 3D printed mask skeleton consisting of four interconnected PLA plastic pieces. This newer skeleton mask was designed to be more stable and comfortable. The third and final form factor was constructed out of a wire frame attached to four 3D printed connectors. We created the wire design after struggling to accommodate different face shapes and sizes with the plastic mask. We first tried solving this issue by printing out several plastic attachments of various sizes so that the mask could be snapped together with custom sized parts to fit a specific user. This worked on some people, but the fit was still rarely ideal. Therefore we decided to switch to a wire frame for increased flexibility and rigidity. The wire frame is very quick and cheap to make and once it is

fitted to a particular face, it maintains its form quite well. However, it takes approximately 5 minutes to

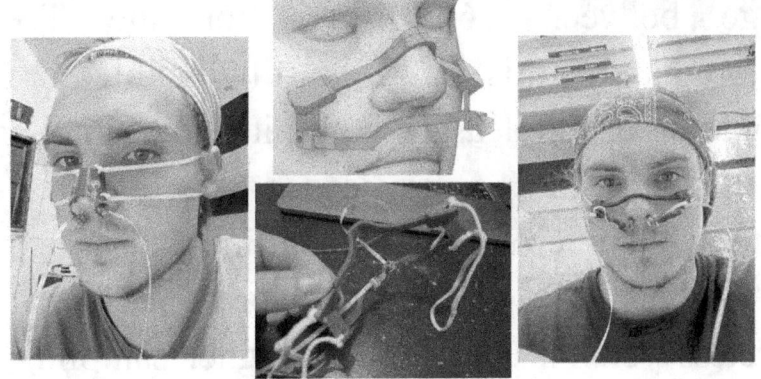

fit a mask to a first-time user.

Figure 5: The three phases of the mask form factor from left to right (nose cap, plastic mask, wire mask)

Hardware

In the earlier stages of the project, we collected data using a Teensy microcontroller and a microSD card. The Teensy was connected to a commercial microphone (ICS-43434) and speaker (OWR-05049T-38D), housed by our form factor. However, the Teensy sampling rate was limited to 44.1 kHz due to hardware constraints. In order to leave an adequate safety margin, we selected a frequency range between 16-20 kHz for the Teensy. Unfortunately, this range is still audible to most people as an unpleasant high-pitch buzzing sound. Furthermore, the Teensy needed to be tethered to a laptop via a micro USB cable during data collection. To address both issues, we transitioned over to a wireless version capable of a higher sampling rate of 50 kHz before conducting pilot studies. This allowed us to reach a higher (inaudible) frequency range of 19-23 kHz. The new hardware consisted of a custom PCB with a BLE (Bluetooth Low Energy) microcontroller connected to the same commercial microphone and speaker. The module, powered by a small 3.7V lithium battery, transmitted data wirelessly to an android phone running a custom app. We used the max98357A audio amplifier to convert digital signals to analog.

Figure 6: Teensy® 4.1 microcontroller on the left, and our custom PCB with BLE microcontroller on the right [8]

Signal Processing

The hardware generates frequency-modulated-continuous-waves (FMCW). FMCW is a well known active acoustic sensing method where an acoustic signal oscillates within a frequency range by steadily increasing in frequency then suddenly dropping back down. The microphone picks up the reflected signals after a short delay, which depends on the distance of surrounding objects. A sliding window then calculates a cross-correlation array for each pair of points in a given frame. Each frame array can then be arranged as a separate column, stacked side by side vertically to create an "echo profile", where the X axis is time and the Y axis represents reflection intensity at various distances. For gesture recognition, it is helpful to focus on only the changing parts of the echo profile and ignore constant reflections. To visualize these changes, we derived a differential echo profile from the original echo profile by subtracting each previous frame from the next. In our implementation, a single frame (or oscillation) is 12 ms (see figure 7).

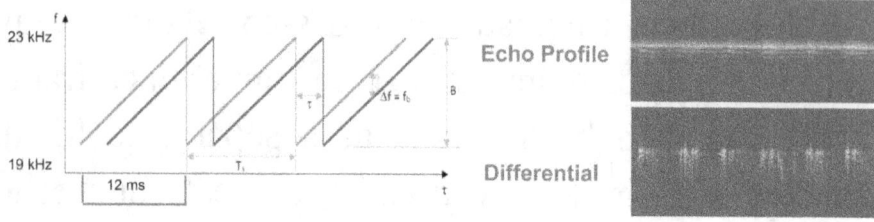

Figure 7: FMCW signal graph - red is the output signal, blue is the reflected signal. Echo profiles are generated from FMCW signals and display time on the X axis and distance on the Y axis. [9]

Preliminary Experiments

To explore the feasibility of the theory of operation, we conducted three preliminary experiments with our wearable device. The first experiment tested whether or not pinching the nose would obstruct the acoustic signals, to verify that signals were indeed passing through the nose. The second experiment explored various sensor positions and orientations. In the third experiment, we generated echo profiles for silently uttered phonemes.

Nose Pinching Experiment

Figure 8 depicts a nose pinching experiment, which a researcher conducted to visualize what would happen to the acoustic signals when the nose was pinched while (1) continuously wiggling the tongue up and down and (2) breathing. Note that the lungs are connected to the oral cavity and subsequently the nasal cavity. Breathing changes the shape of the lungs, which appears to change the way signals propagate through the nose as well. As displayed in figures 9 and 10, results from the experiment showed that plugging the nose does appear to obstruct the acoustic signals, thereby demonstrating the feasibility of using the nose as a gateway into the oral tract.

Figure 8: Pinching the nose while collecting data

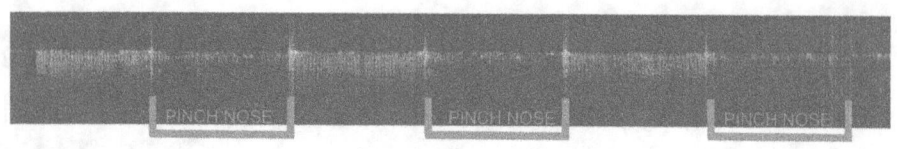

Figure 9: Continuously tapping tongue tip against roof of mouth with mouth closed, and periodically pinching nose

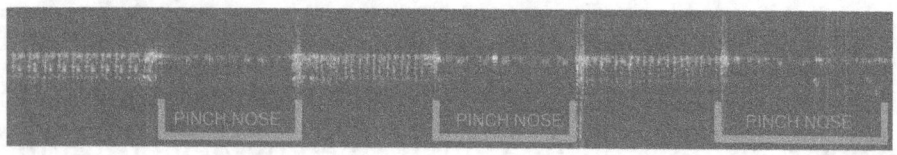

Figure 10: Continuously breathing rapidly through the mouth, and periodically pinching nose

Microphone and Speaker Position Experiment

We later conducted a second experiment testing various positions of the acoustic sensors to further visualize the nasal cavity effect. Figure 11 shows signals from four separate data collection sessions. Throughout each session, the researcher continuously repeated 6 tongue gestures (described later in figure 14). The four sessions had the following sensor orientations:

(1) sensors nearly touching the nose, (2) sensors ~4mm away from the nose, (3) sensors ~4mm away from the nose with nose plugged, (4) sensors placed between the eyes. The strongest differential signals appeared when the speaker and microphone were closest to the nostril openings. As the speaker and microphone moved further away from the nose, the signals weakened. When the nose was then plugged, signals became even fainter. Lastly we positioned the sensors above the nose near the eyes, and the signals nearly disappeared.

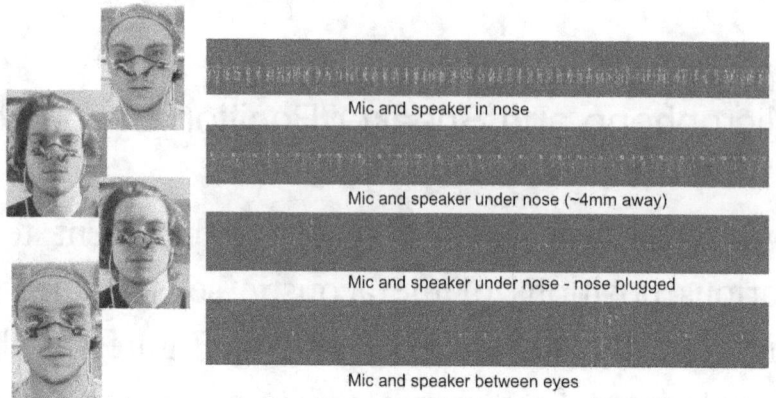

Figure 11: Four different orientations of the acoustic sensors to demonstrate the nasal cavity effect

Phoneme Experiment

In a third experiment, a researcher generated echo profile differentials for three separate utterances of 11 different phonemes (see figure 12). Notice the long vertical tails, representing signal attenuations across a variety of distances. Visually, each phoneme appears rather unique, and separate utterances of the same phoneme appear relatively similar. These preliminary results showed significant promise, justifying further experimentation.

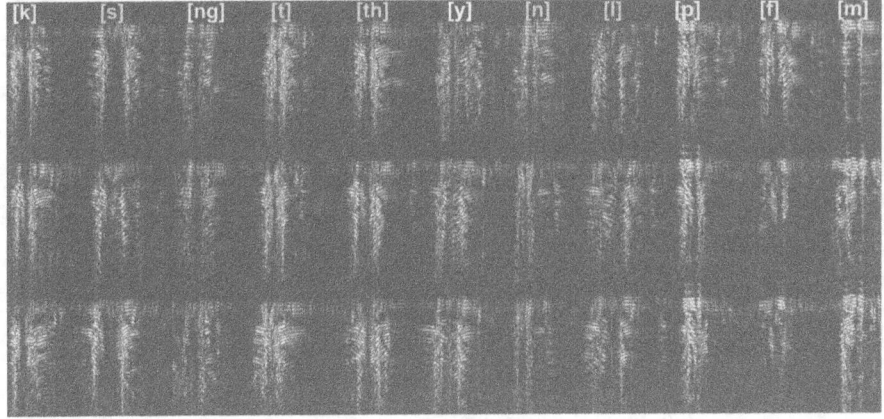

Figure 12: An echo profile differential of 11

different phonemes uttered 3 times each (represented by the 3 rows)

Section 8 : EMA Experiment - Continuously Tracking Speech Articulators

Obtaining a ground truth for continuous tongue tracking is a difficult challenge. Unlike other articulators such as the lips and jaw, tongue movement is mostly hidden from view outside the mouth. One extreme option would be to use an MRI machine to get a full ground truth of the oral tract in high resolution. However, we didn't have access to an MRI machine for research, and even if we did, it would most likely cause too much interference for the Nose Interface to work properly. Instead, we gained access to an Electromagnetic Articulograph (EMA) machine, which is able to track the three dimensional position of five key oral articulators - tongue tip, tongue body, upper lip, lower lip, and jaw. However, the process is rather invasive. To capture the point of each articulator in 3 dimensions, small transducers attached to wires must be applied to each articulator inside the mouth using dental glue. Once the sensors are secured, a large electromagnet is placed next to the user's head. Electromagnetic waves then induce a current in the transducers, sending electrical signals through the wires. Based on the strength of the electrical signals, the EMA machine is able to position each articulator within an accuracy of < mm for 98% of dynamic positional errors (Berry 2011).

A Background on Speech Articulators

Speech on a low level does not merely consist of individual sounds, or phonemes, stringed together in sequence. A more accurate way of characterizing speech production is through the asynchronous movement of speech articulators. For instance, the /b/ in "boot" and "beat" are significantly different sounds. In "boot", the /b/ lip closure is made with rounded lips, while in "beat" the /b/ lip closure is made with retracted lips. This is because the brain anticipates the next sound of the word (/u/ in "boot" or /i/ in "beat") and starts moving the lips into position for the next vowel before the "previous" sound /b/ is even uttered.

EMA Data Collection Experiment

To evaluate the feasibility of the nose interface in tracking speech articulators, we conducted an experiment with an electromagnetic articulograph (see figure 13). In this experiment, a researcher simultaneously collected data from the EMA machine and the nose interface, while uttering words and performing tongue movements. Metal is prone to interfering with EMA signals, so we opted to use a fully 3D printed form factor for the experiment, rather than the standard wire form factor design. The goal of the experiment was to explore to what degree (if any) our system could predict continuous speech articulator movement, when compared against the EMA ground truth data. The tongue, being mostly hidden from view, is one of the most challenging speech articulators to track. To the best of our knowledge, this is the first time that a fully outside-the-mouth wearable device has attempted to predict continuous tongue movement.

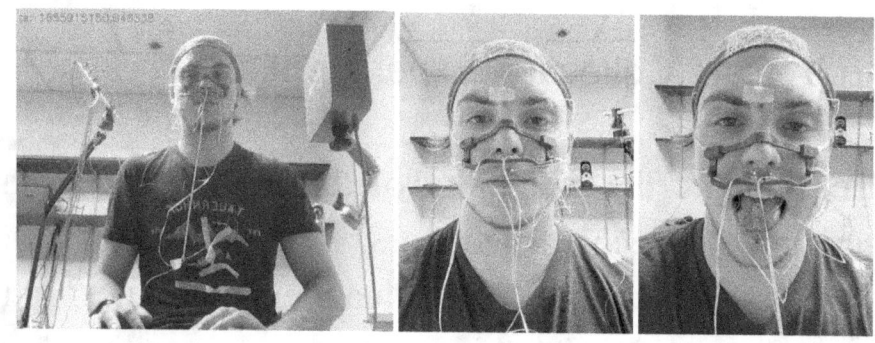

Figure 13: Researcher connected to the EMA machine while wearing a plastic mask form factor

Speech Gestures for EMA Data Collection

The main goal in selecting speech gestures for this experiment was to capture a broad range of movements across the four speech articulators measured by the EMA machine (lower lip, jaw, tongue tip, tongue body), with a focus on tongue-specific sounds. The final gesture set consisted of two parts divided into two separate sessions: a wordlist session and a tongue movement session.

Session 1 - Wordlist

In the wordlist session, the researcher mouthed the following words in sequence while collecting continuous EMA data for ground truth. The wordlist contained the following 11 words: "echo", "Newfoundland", "sing", "lake", "amazing", "alligator", "bedding", "homemade", "afternoon", "Manitoba", and "shy".

Session 2 - Tongue movement

The tongue is the most complex and arguably the most important speech articulator. To further evaluate our system we decided to specifically target tongue tip movement in the second session. Tongue tip tracking could also be used for many continuous input applications beyond speech, such as controlling a wheelchair or a cursor on a screen with the tongue. We derived 6 tongue tip gestures based on Tongueboard (R. Li 2019), each repeated 10 times in random order. To assist in performing the gestures in a consistent manner, the researcher followed a UI animation while collecting EMA data displaying the tongue moving from an inside-the-mouth perspective (similar to Figure 14). The 6 gestures include: "tap", "double tap", "swipe left", "swipe right", "swipe back", "swipe forward" (see figure 14).

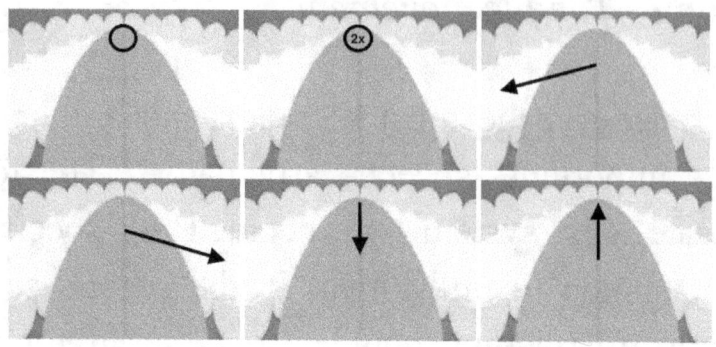

Figure 14: Six tongue gestures (using the tongue tip): 1) tap alveolar ridge, 2) double tap alveolar ridge, 3) slide back along palate, 4) slide forward along palate, 5) slide left along alveolar ridge, 6) slide right along alveolar ridge.

Experiment Procedure

The full EMA experiment was conducted by two researchers with the help of an advisor (EMA operator) and lasted for about 2 hours. One researcher (referred to as the experimenter) helped to secure the sensors, manage the laptop UI and assure all the various wires involved did not tangle. The other researcher was the experiment participant.

Instrumenting the Mouth

First, the researcher sat down on a stool, and the experimenter positioned the EMA electromagnet next to the researcher's head. Next, the experimenter secured eight sensors connected to wires to the researcher using dental glue. Of the eight sensors, three were positioned on the researcher's head (two behind the ears and one on my forehead). These three sensors provide an offset for head movement to the other remaining sensors. The remaining five sensors were attached to 5 key articulators - upper lip, lower lip, jaw, tongue tip, and tongue body. Our speaker caused electromagnetic interference in the upper lip sensor (the closest sensor to the wearable device) resulting in unstable data. For this reason we were forced to exclude the upper lip sensor from our dataset. This left us with 4 remaining working sensors: lower lip, jaw, tongue tip, and tongue body.

Data Collection

Once the sensors were secured to the researcher, the EMA operator and the experimenter coordinated each session to ensure that both EchoNose and the articulograph collected data during the same window of time. For the word list, a new word appeared as text on the screen every 3 seconds. Each word was repeated 10 times in random order, lasting a total of 330 seconds. For the tongue gestures, tongue animation videos (see figure 14) guided the researcher through each gesture. Each tongue gesture lasted for a duration of 4 seconds and was also repeated 10 times in random order, lasting a total of 240 seconds.

Data Processing - Continuous Tracking

The EMA machine provided 3 axes of data (X, Y, and Z) for each of the 4 working sensors (lower lip, jaw, tongue tip, tongue body) leaving us with a total of 12 axes of data. For each session we chose a subset of axes most relevant to that session to analyze - 6 axes from the wordlist session and 3 axes from the tongue movement session.

Session 9 - Wordlist Axes Extraction

Of the 12 axes, we extracted 6 in particular that were especially relevant to speech production. The 6 axes include: one axis for lower lip movement (X axis - forward / back), one axis for jaw movement (Z axis - up / down), two axes (X and Z) for tongue tip movement, and two axes (X and Z) for tongue body movement. We ignored the Y axis (side / side movement) due to the fact that speech is symmetrical, meaning side to side movement offers little to no relevant information in recognizing speech.

Session 10 - Tongue Movement Axes Extraction

The goal of the tongue movement session was to predict tongue tip position in 3 dimensions (X, Y and Z). Unlike speech, our tongue gestures do include side to side (Y axis) movement.

Machine Learning Model

The EMA model is a resnet-18 encoder followed by a fully-connected decoder. MSE (mean squared error) loss is used. The model inputs the echo profiles, a numpy array with ground truth data from the EMA machine (converted from Matlab to Numpy) and a configuration file to synchronize the acoustic signals with the EMA ground truth. It's important to note that the ground truth articulatory data is offset by the 3 reference sensors secured to the head in the experiment procedure, prior to being inputted into the model. The model outputs a numpy array containing the predicted points. Output dimension is the number of axes predicted (since we only predict one axis at a time, it's 1).

EMA Results

One way to evaluate our predictions against the EMA ground truth is to calculate the mean average error (MAE) for a particular axis or group of axes for each speech articulator. However, this figure alone contains very little information about the actual performance of our system. For instance, if that particular sensor and axis moved very little throughout the session, it would produce a lower MAE than a sensor and axis with more frequent movement. This is because it's far easier to predict a value with low fluctuation than a value with high fluctuation. Thus, we opted to use line graphs to visualize nose interface predictions against the EMA ground truth.

Session 11 - Wordlist Articulator Predictions

As previously described, for the wordlist session, we extracted 2 axes for the tongue tip, 2 axes for the tongue body, 1 axis for the lower lip and 1 axis for the jaw for continuous tracking. In the following section we present line graphs for each of the above articulator points and axes. In all the graphs, the EMA ground truth values are in blue and EchoNose's predictions are in orange. Some axes for some articulators predicted much smaller fluctuations compared to the ground truth data. We therefore decided to also present a normalized version of each graph. Among those axes with smaller fluctuations, some tracked the ground truth relatively well after normalization, and others still appeared completely random.

SECTION 12 : Tongue Tip

The tongue tip was perhaps the best performing articulator in the wordlist session. The tongue tip X axis boasts strong predictions, deviating very little from the ground truth even without any normalization. Tongue tip Z appears slightly weaker, but still tracks all the key spikes in the correct direction without normalization. After normalization, the Z axis approximates the ground truth quite well.

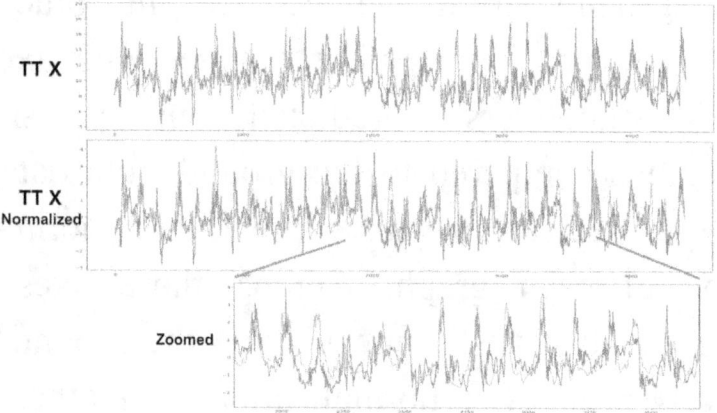

Figure 15: The EMA ground truth (in blue) and EchoNose predictions (in orange) for the X axis of the tongue tip articulator during session 1 (wordlist session) of the EMA experiment

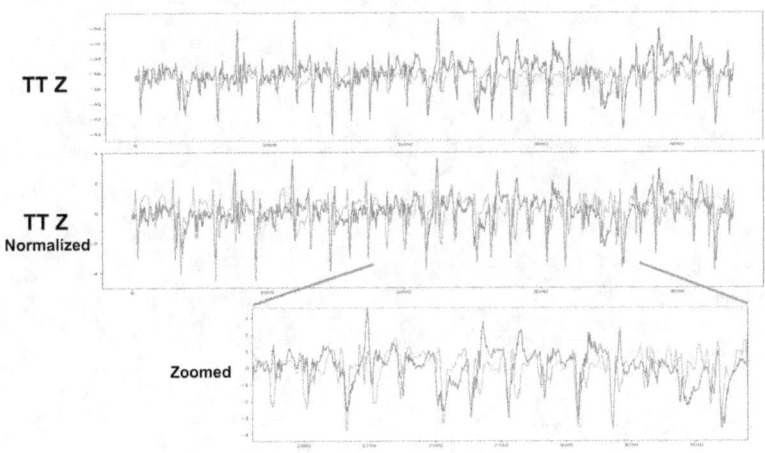

Figure 16: The EMA ground truth (in blue) and EchoNose predictions (in orange) for the Z axis of the tongue tip articulator during session 1 (wordlist session) of the EMA experiment

Tongue Body

Our model struggled to predict both the X and Z axes for the tongue body articulator. However, after normalization, both axes appear to successfully approximate the ground truth to a degree, although the tracing is less apparent compared to the tongue tip

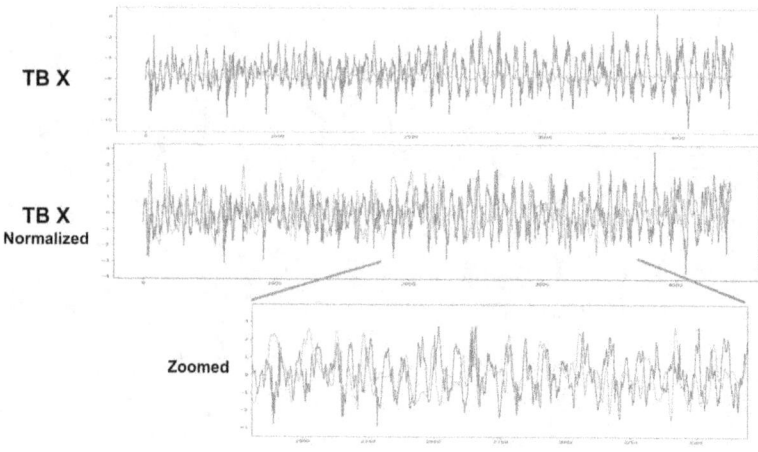

Figure 17: The EMA ground truth (in blue) and EchoNose predictions (in orange) for the X axis of the tongue body articulator during session 1 (wordlist session) of the EMA experiment

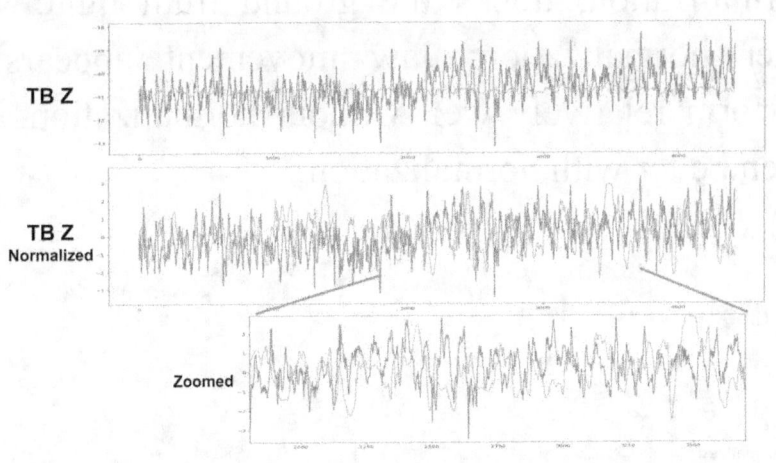

Figure 18: The EMA ground truth (in blue) and EchoNose predictions (in orange) for the Z axis of the tongue body articulator during session 1 (wordlist session) of the EMA experiment

Outside ("visible") articulators - Bottom Lip and Jaw

Unlike tongue movement, lip movement and jaw movement are both clearly "visible" from outside the mouth. Lip movement, although weak before normalization, tracks the ground truth quite well after normalization. Jaw movement appears to perform relatively well without normalization, and even better with normalization.

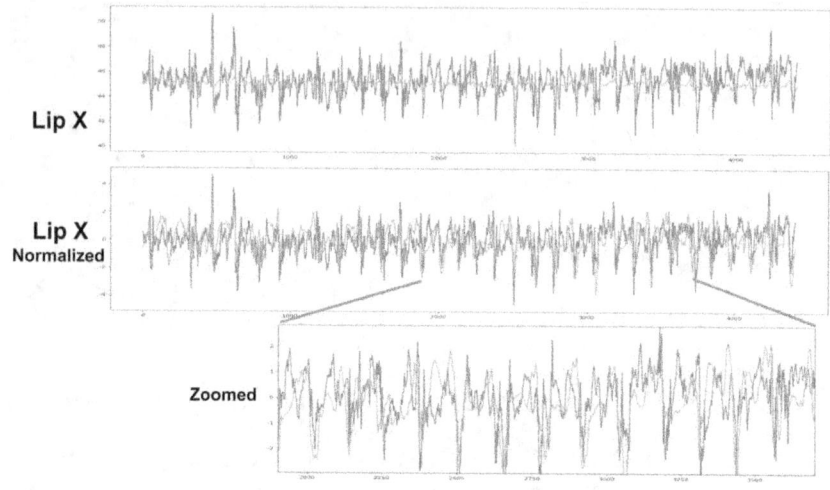

Figure 19: The EMA ground truth (in blue) and EchoNose predictions (in orange) for the X axis of the Lower Lip articulator during session 1 (wordlist session) of the EMA experiment

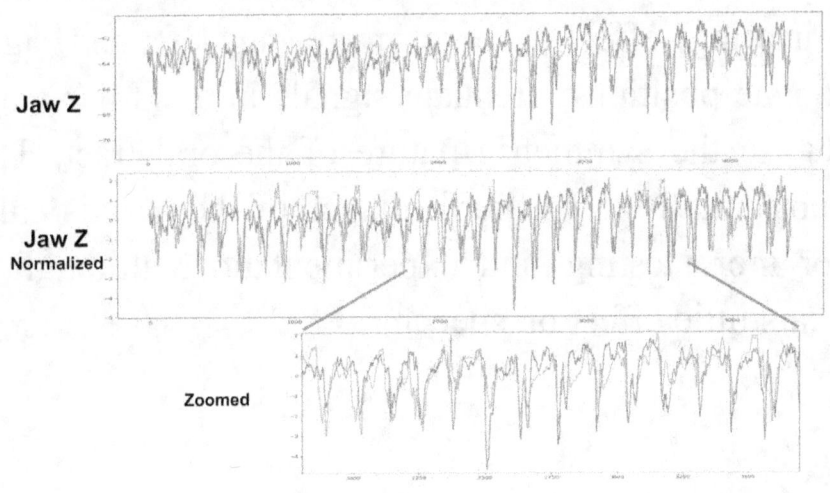

Figure 20: The EMA ground truth (in blue) and EchoNose predictions (in orange) for the Z axis of the jaw articulator during session 1 (wordlist session) of the EMA experiment

Session 2 - Tongue Movement Predictions

The three tongue tip axes predictions did not perform nearly as well as the wordlist predictions. Similarly to the wordlist predictions, the X axis of the tongue tip appears to perform the strongest, followed by the Z axis. Y axis movement fails to be predicted almost entirely, even after normalization. We posit this could be due to a mirroring effect, where mirroring left and right tongue positions attenuate signals in a similar way, due to the symmetric nature of the oral tract. The substantially lower performance of the Y axis calls for more testing and experimentation, although it bears little effect on speech.

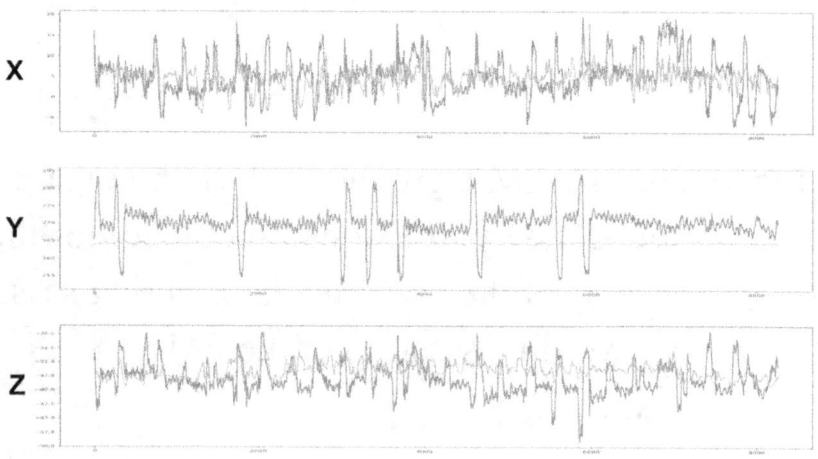

Figure 21: EMA ground truth in blue and model predictions in orange for the X (forward / back), Y (side / side), and Z (up / down) axes of the tongue tip while performing tongue gestures

SECTION 13 : Silent Speech User Study

The EMA continuous tracking showed promise, so we decided to go ahead with a formal user study testing the nose interface's ability to recognize silent speech utterances. First, we conducted a preliminary pilot study to analyze the data and make improvements to the system. Following the pilot study, we made adjustments before proceeding to a full user study.

Preliminary Study

The first preliminary study lasted a total of 90 minutes and consisted of two back-to-back sub-studies. In the first sub-study participants were asked to silently utter 21 words taken verbatim from Tongueboard (R. Li 2019) - 'zero', 'one', 'two', 'three', 'four', 'five', 'six',
'seven', 'eight', 'nine', 'oh', 'add', 'subtract', 'multiply', 'divide', 'percent', 'AM', 'PM', 'hours', 'minutes', and 'seconds'. As previously mentioned in the Related Works section,

Tongueboard is an in-mouth retainer device that, like EchoNose, explores both silent speech recognition and tongue tracking. The Tongueboard wordlist is composed of several smaller wordlists, combined together from previous SSR projects that were foundational in the SSR space. Based on these facts, we decided that Tongueboard's 21-word dataset would serve as an ideal baseline wordlist to evaluate our system. In the second sub-study, participants were asked to silently utter a list of 28 nonwords, each nonword designed to isolate and target a unique phoneme. The 28 nonwords/phonemes included 18 consonants and 12 vowels. Consonants were positioned intervocalically, between two schwas. The schwa is a neutral vowel in English (pronounced "uh"). Schwas involve minimal jaw movement, and a central tongue position, giving each consonant a consistent and relatively neutral phonetic environment. Schwas were written as /a/ on the UI, but participants were instructed to pronounce the /a/

like a schwa sound. Each vowel was isolated between a /b/ and a /t/. The reason for wrapping a phonetic environment around each phoneme was to add consistency to the utterances. If a participant is merely told to utter a vowel sound such as /u/ ("oo"), or a consonant such as /s/, without any context, they may hold these sounds for various durations or vary in pronunciation between utterances (since uttering isolated phonemes is not natural). By providing a consistent phonetic environment, the goal was to improve the repeatability of utterances across sessions and participants.

It is important to note that this was the first experiment conducted on multiple subjects. Like most wearable projects, one of the first challenges we faced in conducting a study on real participants was making our form factor adaptable to different face shapes and sizes. The current mask form factor at this point in time was fully 3D printed, and therefore difficult to adjust. It is at this point that we transitioned to the wire mask form factor (described in the "Form Factor Design" section above).

21 words

	P1	P2	P3	P4	P5	AVG
ts12	0.893	82.1%	0.875	84.4%	89.4%	86.5%
ts34	0.929	97.6%	0.917	90.6%	96.3%	93.8%
ts56	0.97	94.0%	0.893	90.0%	91.9%	92.4%
ts78	0.881	91.1%	0.798	93.1%	91.9%	88.8%
AVG	91.8%	91.2%	87.1%	89.5%	92.4%	90.4%

consonants

	P1	P2	P3	P4	P5	AVG
ts12	0.609	0.789	60.9%	54.7%	78.9%	66.9%
ts34	0.664	0.82	69.5%	76.6%	75.0%	73.9%
ts56	0.625	0.93	62.5%	69.6%	79.7%	73.5%
ts78	0.664	0.813	65.6%	75.0%	64.1%	70.5%
AVG	64.1%	83.8%	64.6%	69.0%	74.4%	71.2%

vowels

	P1	P2	P3	P4	P5	AVG
ts12	0.542	0.552	49.0%	34.4%	60.4%	50.6%
ts34	0.677	0.729	53.1%	45.8%	81.3%	64.2%
ts56	0.667	0.823	47.9%	42.7%	80.2%	64.0%
ts78	0.583	0.75	55.2%	41.7%	58.3%	57.7%
AVG	61.7%	71.4%	51.3%	41.2%	70.1%	59.1%

Figure 22: The first preliminary study results with 21 words and 28 phonemes

Results and Observations

The averages across the 5 participants after cross-session validation was 90.4% for the 21 words,

71.2% for the consonants and 59.1% for the vowels. Some of the first sessions and last sessions are noticeably lower across the board (see figure 22). For the first two session results, we attributed this lower performance to the participants' lack of familiarity with the process, resulting in different utterances when compared with later sessions. As a part of this pilot study, we included a short practice session (half the length of a regular session) before beginning the first session. We attributed lower performance in the last two sessions to participants getting tired and slowing down their speech. P3, for instance, slowed down considerably in the last session of the 21 word list experiment. The longer the study duration, the more likely participants are to gettired, shift around or change their utterances. Additionally, in this pilot study, the UI was configured in such a way that allowed participants to skip to the next word after they had finished uttering the current word. P3 and P4 skipped from word to word very quickly, often cutting off the end of a word mid-utterance. This fast skipping also did not always give their mouth a chance to reach a neutral position between utterances, adding even more variability to the start of the next word. Lastly, some participants struggled with the phonemes, pronouncing the same nonword differently across utterances. Furthermore, not all participants were native speakers, which may have affected the way some phonemes were pronounced.

Adjustments made

We addressed the above issues with the following solutions.

Low performance in the early sessions - we doubled the length of the practice session to allow users to gain more familiarity with the data collection process before beginning the first session

Low performance in the later sessions - we shortened the study to 60 minutes and changed its format to accommodate the shorter duration

Skipping issue - we removed the ability for users to skip to the next word and added a moving karaoke styled progress bar to each word for increased temporal consistency across each utterance

Inconsistent phoneme pronunciation - we removed the phoneme nonword list and instead infused 10 phonetically similar words into the 21 word list (described in more detail in the following section - "User Study Design")

User Study Design

The user study was structured differently than the pilot study. Instead of conducting two separate back to back sub-studies (one for words and the other for phonemes), we conducted a single study consisting of 31 words. This cut the study time from 90 minutes to 60 minutes, which helped to address the issues of participant fatigue and phoneme pronunciation difficulty. The 31 words are composed of two subgroups: (1) the original 21 words from Tongueboard (R. Li 2019) and (2) an additional 10 words chosen to specifically target tongue sounds. The 21 words and the 10 words were mixed together during data collection, and extracted separately later during data processing. Participants were unaware of the two groupings.

The core idea behind this user study design was to evaluate our system's silent speech recognition capabilities beyond what's possible with a function-centered word list. Most word lists in the field are phonetically arbitrary. While previous works in the SSR space have successfully recognized word lists ranging from 10 to 100+ words in length, these wordlists are usually centered around functionality or semantics (such as an application or a theme), rather than phonetics. This approach may test whether speech can be tracked on a high level, but it fails to evaluate the potential scalability of the system. A more thorough evaluation would test how the system would perform distinguishing between more fine grained components of speech, such as phonemes or speech articulators themselves. Consider the following two very short wordlists:

Wordlist 1 - ["Incredible", "cat", "amazing"] Wordlist 2 - ["take", "late", "lane"]

Evidently, the first wordlist should be much easier for any SSR system to classify than the second word list. This is because, unlike the second list, words in the first list are very dissimilar from one another. They vary in syllable count, number of phonemes and diversity of phonemes. This would provide a machine learning model with more clues about each gesture, thus improving performance.

10 Tongue Words

The 10 phonetically-similar words were designed to isolate sounds specific to the tongue (and glottis for h sound). This is because the tongue, unlike the lips or jaw, is relatively hidden from view during speech (although the tongue can still sometimes be seen with open lips). The tongue is the primary speech articulator and the most flexible human muscle capable of movement across many degrees of freedom. It is involved in the production of all vowels and most consonants. Any SSR system incapable of distinguishing between tongue sounds, would be severely limited in its ability to detect speech. Therefore to test EchoNose's performance on words composed of "hidden" phonemes we crafted a list of 10 words (see figures 23 and 24). The words excluded four types of "visible" outside-the-mouth phonemes:

labials - /m/, /p/, /f/

rounded lip sounds - /u/, /oh/, /w/, /r/, /sh/, /dz/

voiced consonant counterparts - /p/ ~~/b/~~, /t/ ~~/d/~~, /k/ ~~/g/~~, /f/ ~~/v/~~, /s/ ~~/z/~~

open vowels - ~~/a/~~, ~~/o/~~, etc.

Group together tongue tip + tongue body/back **(hidden phonemes)**

	Bilabial	Labiodental	Dental	Alveolar	Alveopalatal	Palatal	Velar	Glottal
Stop	p ~~b~~			t ~~d~~			k ~~g~~	~~ʔ~~
Fricative		f ~~v~~	θ ~~ð~~	s ~~z~~	ʃ ~~ʒ~~			h
Affricate					~~tʃ~~ ~~dʒ~~			
Nasal	m			n			ŋ	
Liquid				l, ~~r~~				
Glide	(w)					j	~~(w)~~	

Figure 23: "Hidden" tongue consonants used to create the 10 word list (non-crossed out consonants located in the blue and green boxes) - /t/, /th/, /s/, /n/, /k/, /l/, /y/, /ng/, /h/

Outside vs Hidden Phonemes

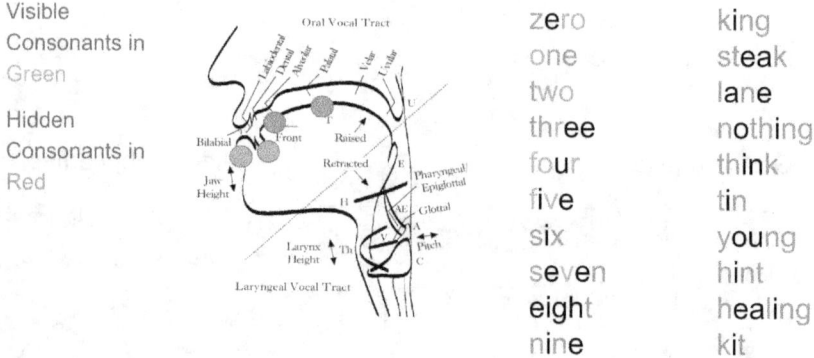

Visible Consonants in Green

Hidden Consonants in Red

zero — king
one — steak
two — lane
three — nothing
four — think
five — tin
six — young
seven — hint
eight — healing
nine — kit

Figure 24: Phoneme distribution of the 10 digits (a subset of the 21 word list) and the 10 phonetically similar words. Visible phonemes appear in green, and map to lip and jaw movement. Hidden phonemes appear in red, and map to tongue movement (and the glottis for /h/).

CV Comparison

We expected our model to perform worse on the 10 hidden phoneme words than the 21 function words, since they were designed specifically to be more phonetically similar. If all the words were equally challenging to recognize, we would actually expect the 10 words to perform better than the 21 words, simply because the wordlist is shorter. However, a lower performance for the 10 words may suggest that hidden phonemes are more difficult to recognize, but it would not prove that our system can in fact detect hidden speech articulators better than other methods. Therefore, to provide a baseline comparison for both the 10 words and the 21 words, we also recorded each session with a frontal camera to later compare against the more traditional CV "lipreading" approach.

User Study Procedure

Six participants took part in the user study. Each study had a duration of approximately 60 minutes, and consisted of 8 consecutive data collection sessions (4 minutes each) with remounting in between. In the study, participants were asked to silently utter or "mouth" words prompted by a UI, while being recorded with a frontal facing camera. We particularly asked the participants to mouth each word naturally, and avoid excessive mouth movement. The wordlist consisted of 31 words total - 21 function words from Tongueboard (R. Li 2019), and the 10 linguistically selected words described in the previous section. We trained and classified the 21 words and the 10 words separately. For each word list, we generated classification results using both the acoustic signals and the frontal camera for comparison.

Machine Learning

EchoNose Classification Model

The classification model we used for the EchoNose results is a resnet-18 CNN encoder with a fully connected decoder. Cross-entropy loss is used for classification. The output dimension is 21 or 10 (depending on the commandset).

CV Classification Model

The CV classification model is a resnet-18 CNN encoder followed by two layers of bi-directional LSTM as temporal feature extractor. Every image frame goes through the encoder separately before going through the LSTM layers. Samples from different utterances are zero-padded to the same length. Finally, a fully-connected decoder is attached after the LSTM layers to predict the speech command. The output dimension is 21 or 10 (depending on the commandset).

User Study Results

For our final results, we calculated cross-session validation across all 8 sessions by averaging the accuracies of four testing groups: sessions 1 and 2, sessions 3 and 4, sessions 5 and 6, and sessions 7 and 8 (see figures 25 and 29). Across the 6 participants, Echonose achieved an average cross-session accuracy of 90.3% on the 21 wordlist, and 84.7% on the 10 "hidden phoneme" words. The frontal camera CV method achieved an average cross-session accuracy of 72.7% on the 21 wordlist, and 51.4% on the 10 wordlist. Both EchoNose and CV performed worse on the 10 "hidden phoneme" words than the 21 wordlist. However, this drop in performance was larger for CV (21.3% drop) than for EchoNose (5.6% drop). We ran a one-way ANOVA test on both the 21 words and the 10 words comparing EchoNose performance against CV performance. EchoNose outperformed CV for the 21 words ($F(1,10) = 5.5134$, $p = 0.0408$)

and substantially outperformed CV for the 10 words ($F(1,10) = 9.6512$, $p = 0.0111$). These results reinforce the idea that CV is weaker at recognizing "hidden" speech sounds involving tongue movement over "visible" speech sounds involving lip movement or high jaw movement. This section consists of an analysis of EchoNose results, followed by a comparison against CV performance.

EchoNose Results

In the following section we analyze EchoNose's performance across the 6 participants and 2 wordlists, and discuss various patterns and abnormalities in the data. Figure 25 below presents EchoNose performance across all 6 participants for each testing group, with averages along the perimeter. Figure 26 displays confusion matrices for the combined average performance across all participants and testing groups.

21 words

	P1	P2	P3	P4	P5	P6	AVG
ts12	97.0%	58.9%	81.5%	73.2%	93.5%	92.3%	82.7%
ts34	98.8%	91.7%	97.0%	95.8%	94.6%	97.0%	95.8%
ts56	98.2%	92.3%	91.1%	99.4%	92.3%	93.5%	94.5%
ts78	92.3%	79.8%	82.7%	92.9%	95.8%	85.7%	88.2%
AVG	96.6%	80.7%	88.1%	90.3%	94.1%	92.1%	90.3%

10 words

	P1	P2	P3	P4	P5	P6	AVG
ts12	97.5%	57.5%	76.2%	65.0%	86.2%	86.2%	78.1%
ts34	95.0%	78.8%	87.5%	91.2%	96.2%	88.8%	89.6%
ts56	97.5%	67.5%	87.5%	96.2%	95.0%	92.5%	89.4%
ts78	88.8%	62.5%	75.0%	81.2%	97.5%	85.0%	81.7%
AVG	94.7%	66.6%	81.6%	83.4%	93.7%	88.1%	84.7%

Figure 25: EchoNose performance for all 6 participants with cross-session validation. The first column (ts12, ts34, ts56, ts78) indicates which two sessions were used for testing.

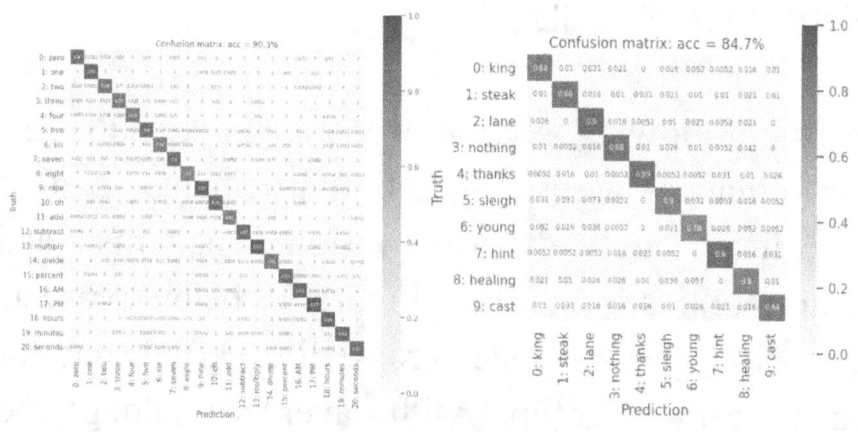

Figure 26: Confusion matrices for average EchoNose performance across all 6 participants

after cross-session validation. The 21 words averaged 90.3% (on the left) and the 10 words averaged 84.7% (on the right).

Lower Performance in the Early Sessions

Participants P2, P4 and P3 (to a lesser extent) performed significantly worse when the first two sessions were used for testing (yellow boxes in figure 25). In the preliminary study we noticed a similar effect, and attributed lower results in the first two sessions to a lack of user familiarity with the dataset. We previously addressed the issue by lengthening the practice session. Unfamiliarity with the data collection process can lead to increased temporal variation in those particular sessions, causing our model to be confused. Although this may have helped boost performance in the early sessions, it ultimately failed to resolve the issue in its entirety. After reviewing frontal camera recordings from P2 and P4, we realized that for certain nose shapes in the early sessions, the mask form factor would slowly slide up the face (pulled by the elastics around the ear). Once the mask is acclimated or "broken in" to the user's face shape the sliding effect is reduced. Figure 27 is similar to Figure 26, except that it excludes the first testing grouping (session 1 and 2) from the results. This alone boosted performance by 2.5 % for the 21

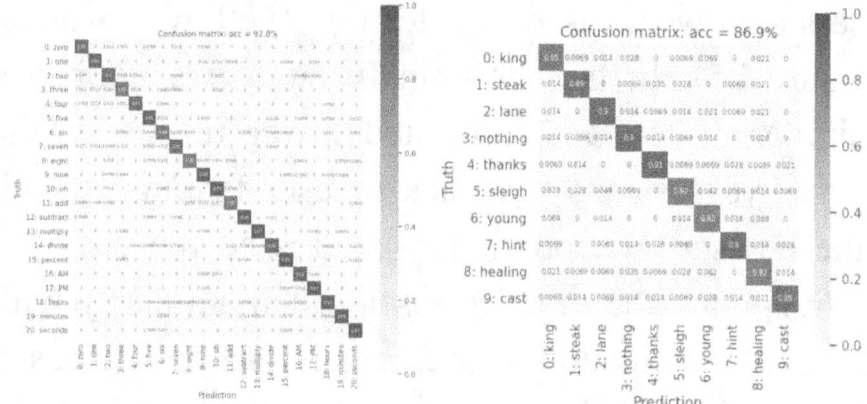

wordlist and 2.2% for the 10 wordlist.

Figure 27: Confusion matrices for average EchoNose performance across all 6 participants after cross-session validation, excluding the first two sessions from testing. The 21 words averaged 92.8% (on the left) and the 10 words averaged 86.9% (on the right).

Variation in Performance across Participants

P2 (and to a lesser degree P3 and P4) achieved lower results than the other participants. This could be due to a few factors. Firstly, we see that all three participants had lower performances when testing sessions 1 and 2 were used for testing. This suggests form factor shifting, as described in the earlier section. Furthermore, participants were instructed to speak naturally and avoid excessive or exaggerated mouth movements during the user study. These participants (P2 in particular) spoke (silently) with extremely minimal mouth movement. Figure 28 shows cropped mouth images of P1 and P2 prior to uttering the word "young" and then again mid-utterance. Notice how P2's echo profile has less temporal information and weaker tails compared to P1. Additionally, P1's mouth movement in the second image is more apparent,

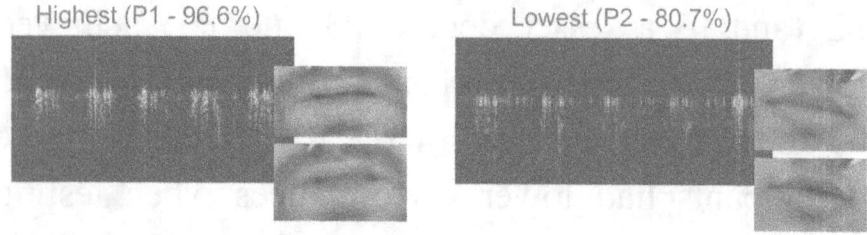

while P2's mouth movement is extremely minimal.

Figure 28: Echo profiles and mouth images showing the start and middle of the utterance "young" for P1 and P2

CV Results Comparison

The CV results fluctuate across participants, with P1 achieving the highest performance on both wordlists and P2 and P6 performing the worst. Unlike EchoNose results, CV results show more consistency across testing sessions for each participant. This indicates that the lower accuracies in the early sessions of the EchoNose results were not due to user behavior, but rather due to form factor shifting and possibly remounting issues between sessions.

21 words

	P1	P2	P3	P4	P5	P6	AVG
ts12	95.8%	54.8%	72.0%	75.0%	85.1%	57.7%	73.4%
ts34	99.4%	57.7%	66.1%	81.5%	85.7%	60.7%	75.2%
ts56	97.6%	55.4%	69.0%	76.2%	79.2%	50.0%	71.2%
ts78	97.6%	46.4%	67.9%	83.3%	85.1%	45.2%	70.9%
AVG	97.6%	53.6%	68.8%	79.0%	83.8%	53.4%	72.7%

10 words

	P1	P2	P3	P4	P5	P6	AVG
ts12	87.5%	31.3%	51.3%	57.5%	58.8%	31.3%	52.9%
ts34	95.0%	28.8%	45.0%	50.0%	48.8%	33.8%	50.2%
ts56	96.3%	25.0%	51.3%	55.0%	52.5%	28.8%	51.5%
ts78	97.5%	28.8%	46.3%	56.3%	57.5%	20.0%	51.0%
AVG	94.1%	28.4%	48.4%	54.7%	54.4%	28.4%	51.4%

Figure 29: Frontal camera CV performance for all 6 participants after cross-session validation. The first column (ts12, ts34, ts56, ts78) indicates which two sessions were used for testing. The 21 words averaged 72.7% and the 10 words averaged 51.4%

Figure 31 displays a comprehensive bar chart comparing performance for EchoNose and CV for both the 21 words and the 10 words. As expected, CV consistently performed worse than EchoNose on the 10 hidden phoneme word list. However, CV also performed significantly worse on the 21 word set (with the exception of P1). We initially expected CV results to be higher than or at least comparable to EchoNose for the 21 words. After analyzing the frontal camera video and observing echo profiles, we attribute this low CV accuracy across the board to minimal mouth movement. In most silent speech user studies, participants are encouraged to clearly enunciate each word. However, in our user study we specifically instructed participants to silently utter each word naturally, resulting in minimal mouth movement. This procedure was especially designed to challenge the CV method. Unlike the other 5 participants, P1 was an outlier in the dataset, performing well across both wordlists for both EchoNose and CV. Figure 30 shows cropped mouth images for all 6 participants before and during the utterance: "young". Notice how P1's mouth is wider and naturally open in the neutral position (top left image). In the middle of the utterance (bottom left image), there are two observations to note: (1) P1's tongue can be seen raising to complete the /y/, and (2) P1's mouth is visibly more open than other participants to produce the vowel. So P1's unusually high CV performance can most likely be attributed to mouth shape and heightened enunciation.

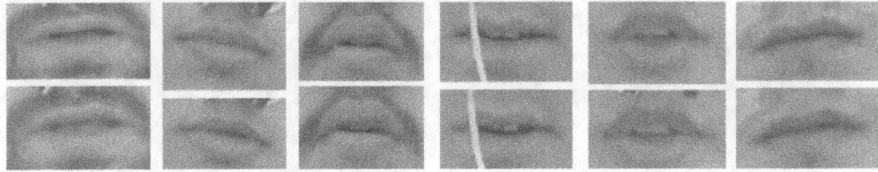

Figure 30: Cropped lips for P1 to P6 (left to right) before and during the word "young"

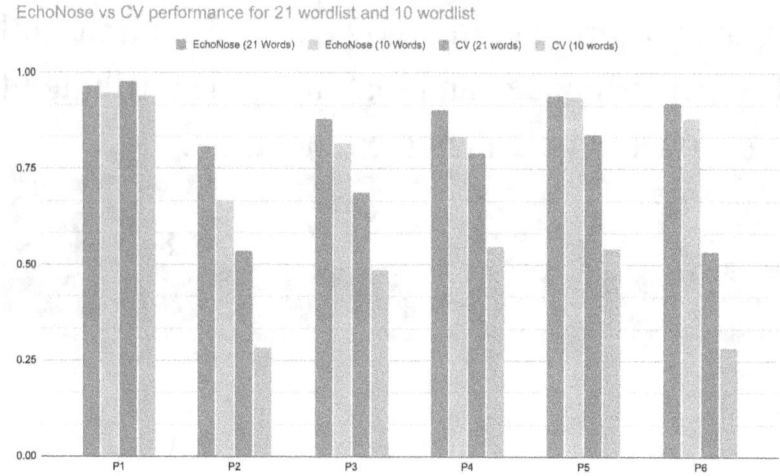

Figure 31: EchoNose (in blue) compared with CV (in red) for the 21 wordlist and the 10 wordlist

Figure 32 displays a differential bar chart derived from figure 31. Take note of P1 and P5 in particular. Although they both share very high EchoNose accuracies, their CV performance gap is quite significant. This appears to be due to the stark difference between mouth movement across both participants. Nevertheless, CV's larger gap between the 10 words overall is apparent.

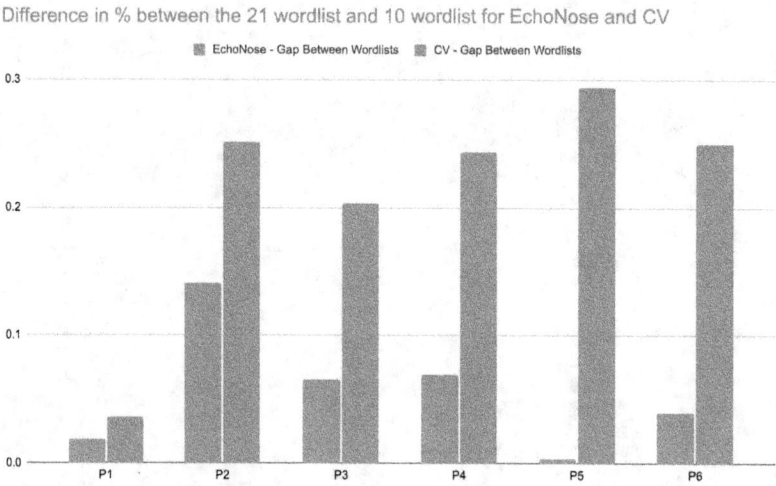

Figure 32: Compares the gap between the 21 word list and 10 word list for EchoNose (in blue) and CV (in red) across all 6 participants

Discussion

Over the course of this work we have demonstrated the feasibility of leveraging the nasal cavity for silent speech recognition and tongue tracking. EchoNose is the first minimally-invasive wearable device known to attempt continuous tongue tracking from outside the mouth. The EchoNose user study was also the first known silent speech study of its kind, designed to isolate "hidden" phonemes to compare against CV. Furthermore, the wearable system is cheap, minimalist and session independent. However, despite encouraging results, there are still limitations to address. Firstly, cross-session performance varies across participants, most likely due to form factor instability. This could be addressed by improving the current mask form factor design, or exploring new form factors such as VR headsets or glass frames, which may offer more stability (see figure 33). Additionally, we could increase the number of participants in future studies and make further improvements to the machine learning models.

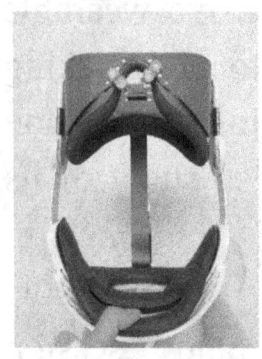 

Figure 33: Preliminary VR form factor design

New sensor variations could also be explored. One possible variation to this design is to instead place the microphone in front of the mouth rather than under a nostril (see figure 34). In this variation the speaker is still positioned under the nose, but now the microphone sits at the mouth's entrance. With this orientation, the speaker propagates acoustic signals through the nasal cavity and the microphone captures them leaving the mouth (similar to vocalized speech). Preliminary results show promise, but more research needs to be conducted. Lastly, other applications beyond silent speech recognition could also be explored using EchoNose (e.g. user authentication, tongue tracking for UI control, eating and drinking detection, speech pathology, or tracking lower respiratory tract activities such as breathing and coughing). Ultimately, any activities involving the respiratory tract changing shape could be explored in the future.

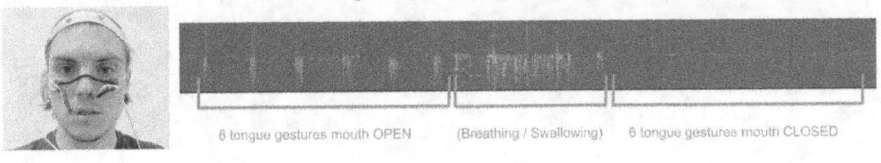

Figure 34: Nose-mouth form factor variation with the mouth open and closed